Enfield Libraries

S

PALMERS GREEN LIBRARY
BROOMFIELD LANE
LONDON N13 4EY
Renewals: 020 8379 2711
Enquiries: 020 8379 2754

10/06

10 NOV 2012

- 8 FEB 2007
- 4 SEP 2008

22 DEC 2008

23 AUG 2011
07 OCT 2011
15 NOV 2011

Please remember that this item will attract overdue charges if not returned by the latest date stamped above. You may renew it in person, by telephone or by post quoting the bar code number and your library card number.

www.enfield.gov.uk

LS131

781.5

* PLEASE CHECK FOR CD
ON BACK COVER!!

Play Piano with...
Ray Charles

Wise Publications
part of The Music Sales Group

London / New York / Paris / Sydney / Copenhagen / Berlin / Madrid / Tokyo

Published by
Wise Publications
8/9 Frith Street, London W1D 3JB, England.

Exclusive Distributors:
Music Sales Limited
Distribution Centre, Newmarket Road,
Bury St. Edmunds, Suffolk IP33 3YB, England.
Music Sales Pty Limited
120 Rothschild Avenue, Rosebery, NSW 2018, Australia.

Order No. AM91964
ISBN 0-7119-4080-0
This book © Copyright 2005 by Wise Publications.

Compiled by Nick Crispin.
Music arranged by Paul Honey.
Cover photograph courtesy of David Redfern/Redferns.
Printed in Great Britain by Printwise (Haverhill) Limited, Haverhill, Suffolk.

CD recorded, mixed and mastered by Jonas Persson.
Piano by Paul Honey.
Bass by Don Richardson.
Drums by Ian Thomas.
Backing vocals by Alison Symons & Cat Hopkins.
Trumpets by Mike Lovatt & Andy Gathercole.
Tenor sax by Howard McGill.
Baritone sax by Colin Skinner.
Strings by Ben Buckton, Susie Candlin, Catherine McCraken & Justin Pearson.

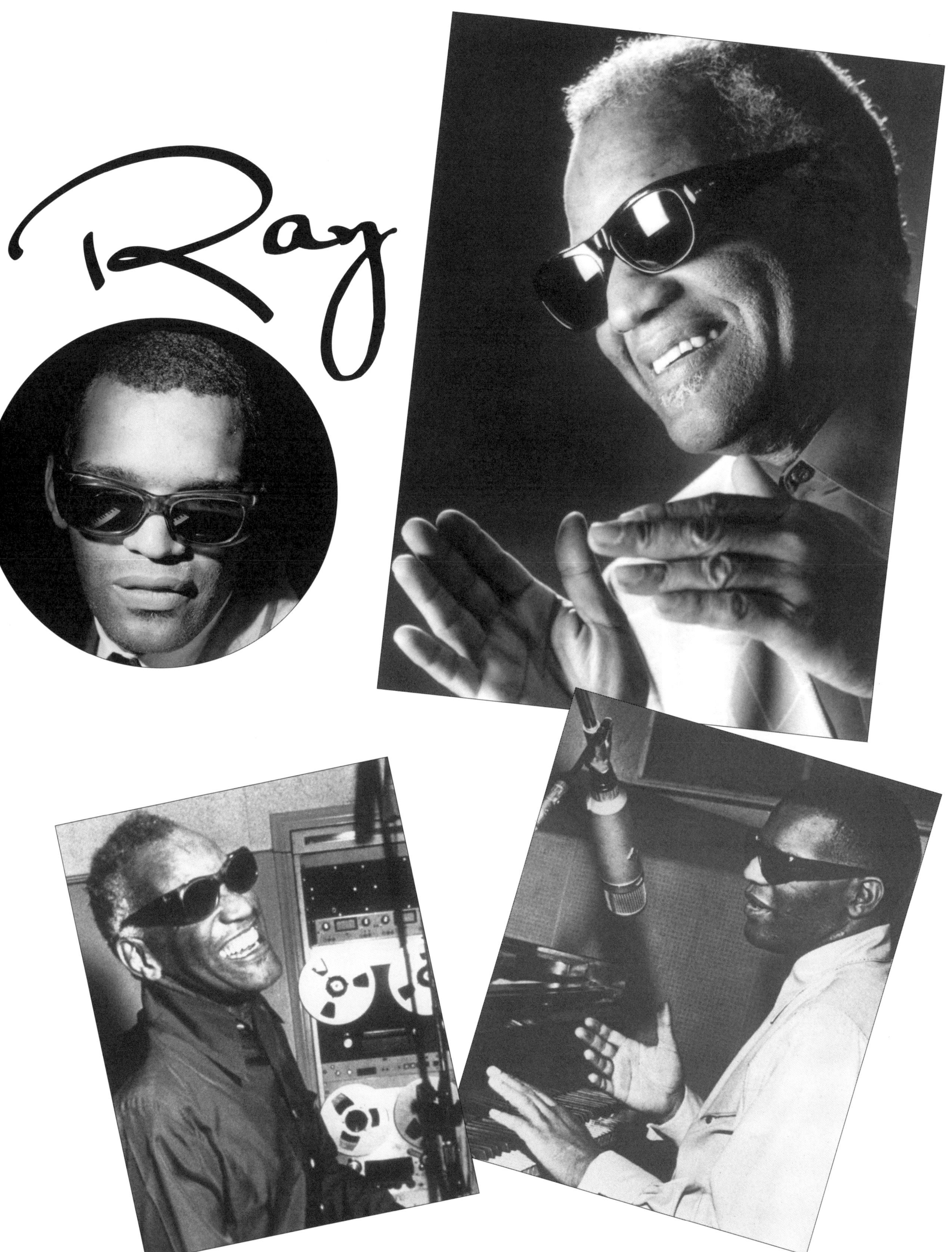
Ray

Drown In My Own Tears

Words & Music by Henry Glover

Eb9
5fr
Ab
4fr
Ab7(#5)
4fr
Ab13
4fr
drown - in' my___ own tears.
I___ sit and cry___
Db
4fr
Ab7(#5)
4fr
Db
4fr
Ab7
4fr
Db
4fr
Db7
just like a child,_______________
my pour - in'
Gb
Gdim
tears_
are run - nin' wild.___
If you don't
Db
4fr
F7
Bbm
Bbm/Ab
Gb
Gdim
think
you'll be home_______ soon,_______
I'll guess I'll
3
3
3
3
3

Db   Bbm   Eb9   Ab7   Db   Gb7   Db7   Db9
drown,__ oh__ yes, in my own tears.__ I know it's
Gb   Gdim
true,_ mm,_ in-to each life, oh__ some
Db   Ab7(#5)   Db   Ab7   Db   Db7
rain,________________ rain__ must pour.__ I'm,__ so__
Gb   Gdim
__ blue   here with-out you,____ it keeps a-

E♭7
A♭7
A♭7(♯5)
rain - in' more and more. Why can't
D♭
D♭9
A♭7(♯5)
D♭
A♭7
D♭
D♭7
you come on home? Ooh yes, so I
G♭
Gdim
won't be all a - lone. If you don't
D♭
F7
B♭m
B♭m/A♭
G♭
Gdim
think you'll be home soon, I guess I'll

Db6
Gb
Db6
Gb
(drown in my own tears),
(drown in my own tears),

Db6
Gb
Db6
Gb
(drown in my own tears),
(drown in my own tears). I guess I'll

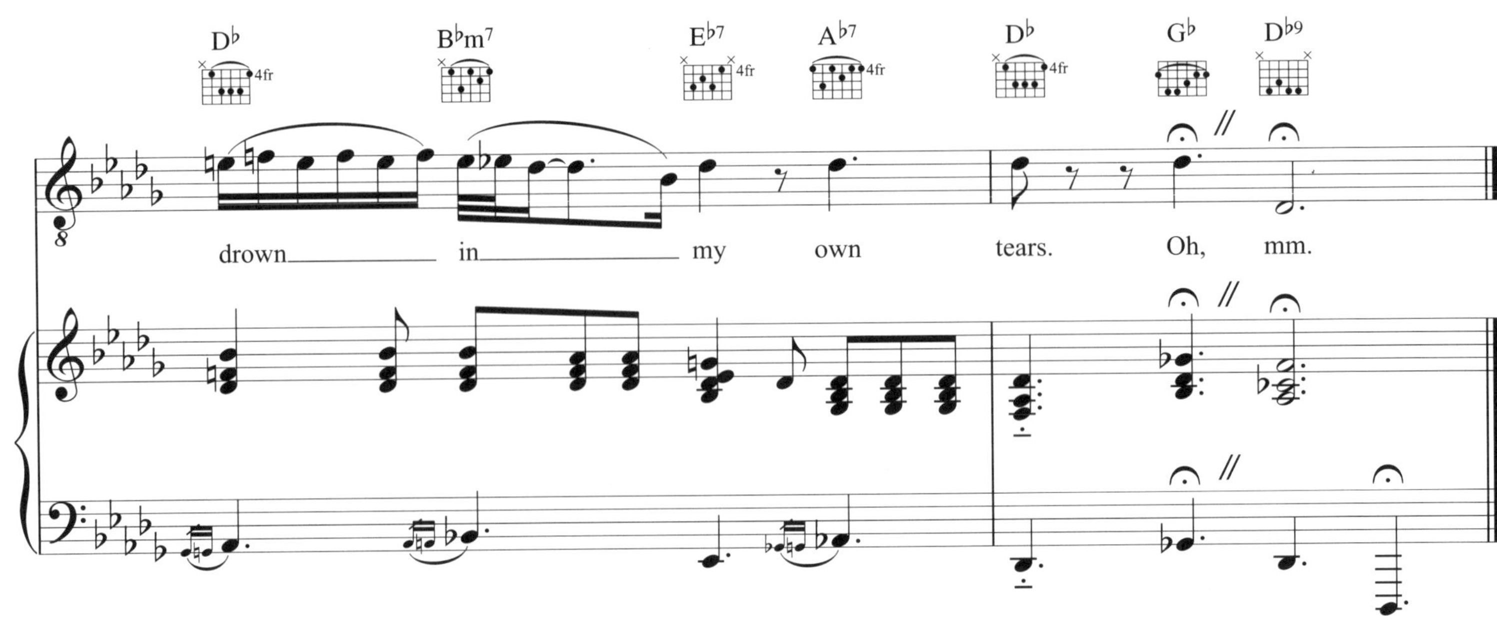

Db
Bbm7
Eb7
Ab7
Db
Gb
Db9
drown in my own tears. Oh, mm.

Georgia On My Mind

Words by Stuart Gorrell
Music by Hoagy Carmichael

1 bar count in

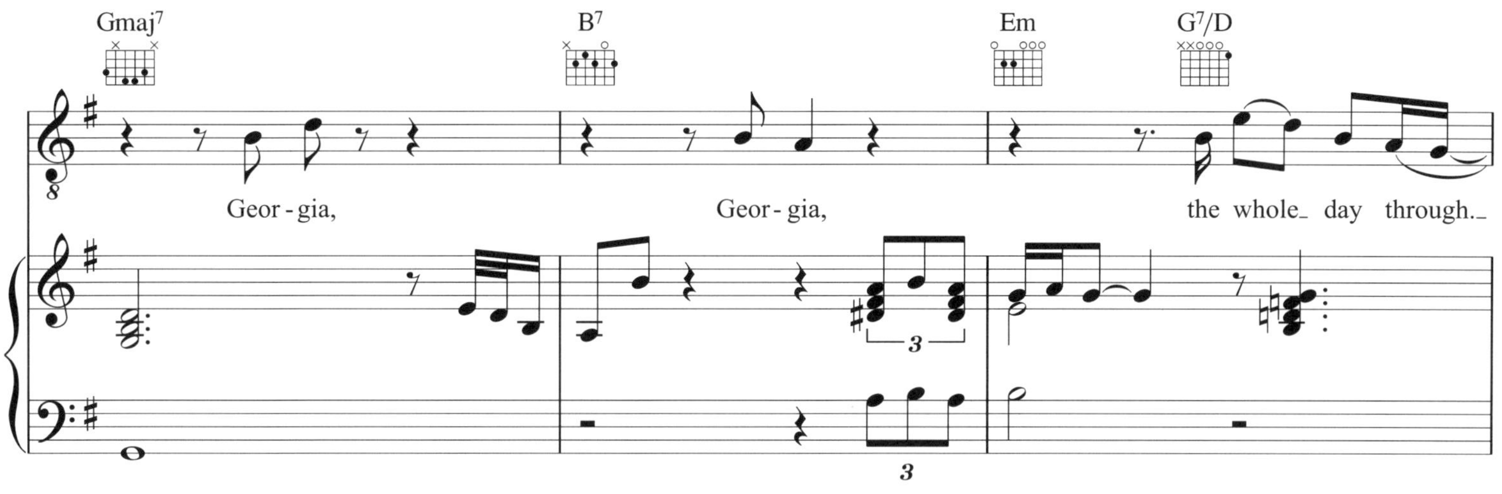

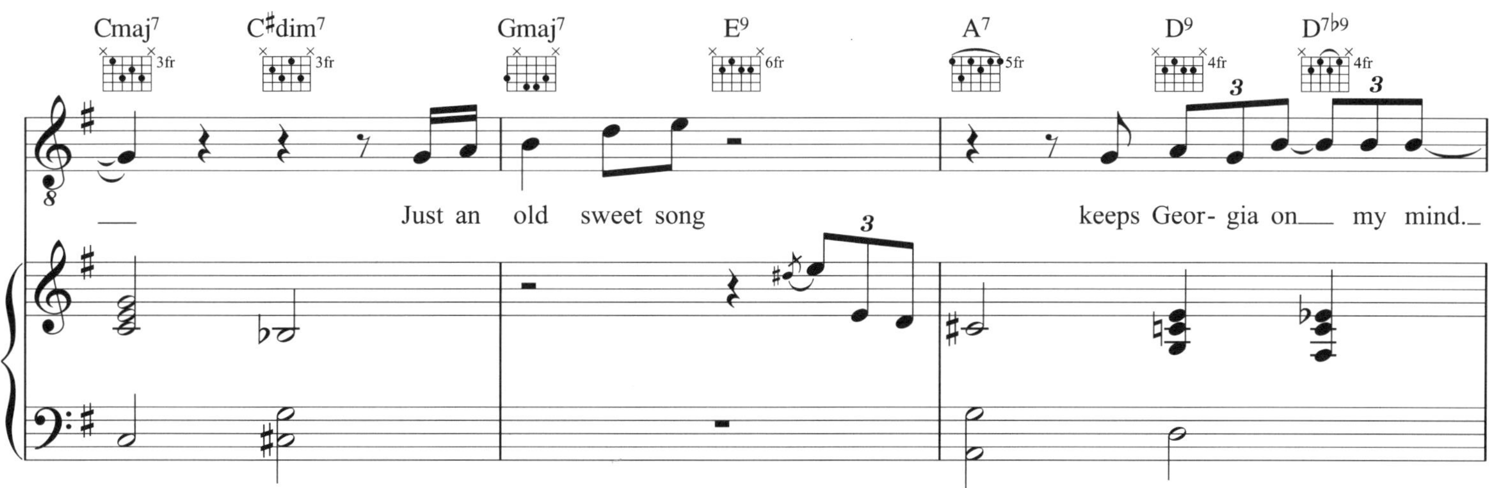

B7b5 E9 A7 D7b9 Gmaj7
I said a - Geor - gia,
B7 Em G7/D Cmaj7 C#dim7
Geor - gia,
a song of you comes
Gmaj7 E9 A7 D9 Gmaj7 C9
as sweet and clear
as moon-light through the pines.
Gmaj7 B7 Em Am7 Em6 C9
O-ther arms reach out to me,

Em   Am7   Em   A7*   Em   Am7
o-ther eyes smile____ ten-der-ly. Still in the peace-ful
Gmaj7   F#7   Bm   Bb7b5   A7*   D9
dreams I see__________ the road leads back to you.__ I said
Gmaj7   B7   Em   G7/D
Geor-gia, woh, Geor-gia,__ no peace_ I__
Cmaj7   C#dim7   Gmaj7   E9   A7   D9
__ find,__ just an old sweet song keeps Geor-gia____ on my

Gmaj7 C9 Gmaj7 B7 Em Am7 Em6 C9
mind.   O-ther arms   reach   out   to   me,
Em Am7 Em A7* Em Am7
o - ther eyes   smile   ten - der - ly.   Still in   peace - ful
Gmaj7 F#7 Bm7 B7b5 A7* D9
dreams   I   see   the road   leads   back   to   you.   Woh,
Gmaj7 B7 Em
Geor - gia,   Geor - gia,   no peace,   no peace

Cmaj7 C#dim7 Gmaj7 E9 A7 D9
I'll find___ just an old sweet song, keeps Geor-gia___ on my
F9 E9 A7
mind.___ I said just an old sweet song___
D9 D7b9 Gmaj7 Cmaj7 C#dim7
keeps Geor - gia on___ my mind.___
Gmaj7 Ab7 G7 G7#9
Freely
8va

Hallelujah I Love Her So

Words & Music by Ray Charles

lives next door.
Ev-'ry morn-ing 'fore the sun comes up
she bring my cof-fee in my fav-'rite cup, that's why I know,________ yes I
know_____ why,_ hal-le-lu-jah I just love her so.
When I'm in trou-ble and I have no friend,_ I know she'll go with me un-

Eb Edim N.C. Bb N.C. Bb7 N.C. Bb7#5
til the end.___ Ev-'ry-bo-dy asks me how I know,___
Eb N.C. Edim N.C. Bb D7
I smile at them and say she told me so. That's why I know,_______ oh_____
Gm Eb7 C7b9 F7 Bb Bb7#5
I know, hal-le-lu-jah I just love her so.
Eb N.C. Edim
Now if I call her on the te-le-phone,

and tell her that I'm all a - lone,
by the time I count from
one to four,
I hear her on my door.
In the eve-ning when the sun go down,
when there is no-bo-dy
else a - round,
she kiss-es me and she hold me tight,

and tell me Dad-dy ev-'ry - thing's all right. That's why I know, yes
I know, hal - le - lu - jah I just love her so.
Sax. solo
To Coda
mf
N.C.
N.C.

D.S. al Coda
Coda
Repeat to fade
N.C.
-lu - jah I just love her so. Oh,______ hal - le -
-lu - jah, don't you know______ I just love her so.

I Can't Stop Loving You

Words & Music by Don Gibson

24

it's use-less to say,____ so I'll just live my life____
in dreams of yes - ter - days.____ Those__ hap - py
hours that we__ once knew, though__ long a - go__
____ they still__ make me blue.____ They__ say__ that

F   F7   Bb
time   heals a bro-ken heart,___   but time has stood

F   C7   F Bb/F   F7   F7#5
still,________   since we've been a-part.________   (I can't stop

Bb   F
lov-ing you),   I've made up my mind,________

Fmaj7   F6   C7   Gm7   C7   F
to live in me-mo-ries________   of the lone-some time.

F7 F7#5 B♭
(I can't stop want - ing you).   It's use - less to
F   Fmaj7 F6 C7
say,____   so I'll just live my life____
Gm7 C7 F B♭/F F
in dreams of yes - ter - days.____   (Those hap - py
F F7 B♭
hours   that we__ once knew,   though long a -

F   C7
go,_______ still make me blue.   They say_____ that
F   F7   Bb
time   heals a bro - ken heart,   but time has stood
F   C7   F Bb   F7   F7#5
still   since we've been a - part.   I can't stop
Bb   F
lov - ing you),   I said I've made up my mind_______

Fmaj7   F6   C7   Gm7   C7   F
to live in me - mo - ries____ all the lone - some time.
F7   F7#5   Bb
(I can't stop want - ing you).   It's use - less to
F   F6   C7   rall.
say,____   so I'll just live my life____
                              F   Bb/F   F
of dreams of yes - ter - days.____

Shake A Tail Feather

Words & Music by Otis Hayes, Andre Williams & Verlie Rice

D
Bm
E7
why didn't you ask__ me ba - by, or did-n't you think__ I could?__

A7
D
G7
__ Well I know___ that the Boo - gi - loo is out of sight, but the

D
G7
D
Shing - a - ling's the thing to - night, but if that were you and me out now ba -

Bm
E7
A7
- by I would have shown you how to do it right,___ do it right,__

do it right,______ do it right,
do it right,___ do it right.______
Aah.______
D
5fr
G7
3fr
D
5fr
Twist - in', shake it, shake it, shake it, shake it, ba - by,______
mf cresc.
gliss.

A7
G7
hey we're gon - na loop - de - loop,
D
D7
G7
shake it up ba - by.___
Hey we're gon - na
A7
loop - de - la,
bend ov - er, let me see you shake your tail - fea - ther,
mf cresc.
bend ov - er let me see you shake your tail - fea - ther,
come on___ let me

see you shake your tail - fea-ther, come on___ let me see you shake your tail - fea-ther.
Aah.___
gliss.
D
Twist - in',
G7
shake it, shake it, shake it, shake it, ba - by,___
D
N.C.
G7
hey we're gon - na loop - de-loop,
D
shake it up

D7   G7   A7
ba - by.___   Hey we're gon-na loop-de-la,   bend ov - er, let me
mf cresc.
see you shake your tail - fea-ther,   bend ov - er let me   see you shake your tail - fea-ther,
come on___   let me   see you shake your tail - fea-ther,   come on___   let me
see you shake your tail - fea-ther. Aah.___   gliss.   Come on.___

D7
G7
D7
G7
Play 4 times
D7
G7
D7
G7
Play 4 times
A7
D7
gliss.
Aah.
Twist - in',
G7
D7
G7
Repeat to fade
shake it, shake it, shake it, shake it, ba - by.

A Song For You

Words & Music by Leon Russell

Ab   Ebsus2/G   Fm7   Eb/G
I've act-ed out my life on sta - ges with ten thou-sand peo - ple watch - ing,__
Ab   Eb/Bb   Bb7sus4   Eb   G7
but we're a - lone__ and I'm just a - sing - ing this song__ for you.
Cm   G7/B
I know your i-mage of me is what I hope to be,____ ba - by.
Cm/Bb   Cm/A
I treat - ed you un-kind - ly but girl,__ can't you see____

A♭ E♭/G Fm⁷ E♭/G
there's no-one more im-por-tant to me.__ So darl-ing can't you please__ see through me
A♭ E♭/B♭ B♭⁷sus⁴ E♭ G⁷
'cos we're a-lone and now I'm__________ sing-ing my song for you.__
Cm G⁷/B Cm/B♭ Cm/A
You taught me pre-cious sec-rets of the truth with-hold-ing no-thing.__
A♭ E♭/B♭ A♭/E♭ E♭ G⁷
You came out in front and I was hid-ing,__ yeah.

Cm
G7/B
Eb/Bb
Cm/A
But now I'm so much bet-ter so if my words don't come to-ge-ther,
Ab
Gm7
F7
Bb7sus4
Bb
lis-ten to the me-lo-dy 'cos my love's in there hid-ing.
N.C.
8va
G7
Cm
G7/B
8va
I love you in a place where there's no space or time,

Cm/B♭
Cm/A
I love you for my life, 'cos you're a friend of mine.
A♭
E♭/G
Fm⁷
E♭/G
And when my life is ov-er re-mem-ber when we walked to-ge-ther,
A♭
E♭/B♭
B♭⁷sus⁴
E♭
we were a-lone and I was sing-ing my song for you.
E♭/D♭
D♭
A♭

Gm7b5
C7
Fm7
Fm7/Eb
Dm7b5
G7#5
G7
I
Cm
G7/B
loved you in a place where there's no space or time,
Cm/Bb
Cm/A
I've loved you for my life, yes, you're a friend of mine.
Ab
Eb/G
Fm7
Eb/G
And when my life is ov - er re - mem-ber when we were to - ge - ther,
ff

Ab   Eb/Bb   Bb7sus4   Eb
we were a-lone and I___ was sing-ing my song___ for you.   Yes,
Ab   Eb/Bb   Bb7sus4   Eb   Ab   Eb/G
we__ were a-lone and I___ was sing-ing this song__ for you.__   Yeah,   we__ were a-lone and I___ was
Db   Ab   3   3   3
sing-ing my song,   sing-ing my song,___   sing-ing my
Ab/Eb   3   Eb   poco rall.   Bb
song,___   sing-ing my song,___   sing-ing my   song.___
8vb

Unchain My Heart

Words & Music by Bobby Sharp & Teddy Powell

2 bars count in

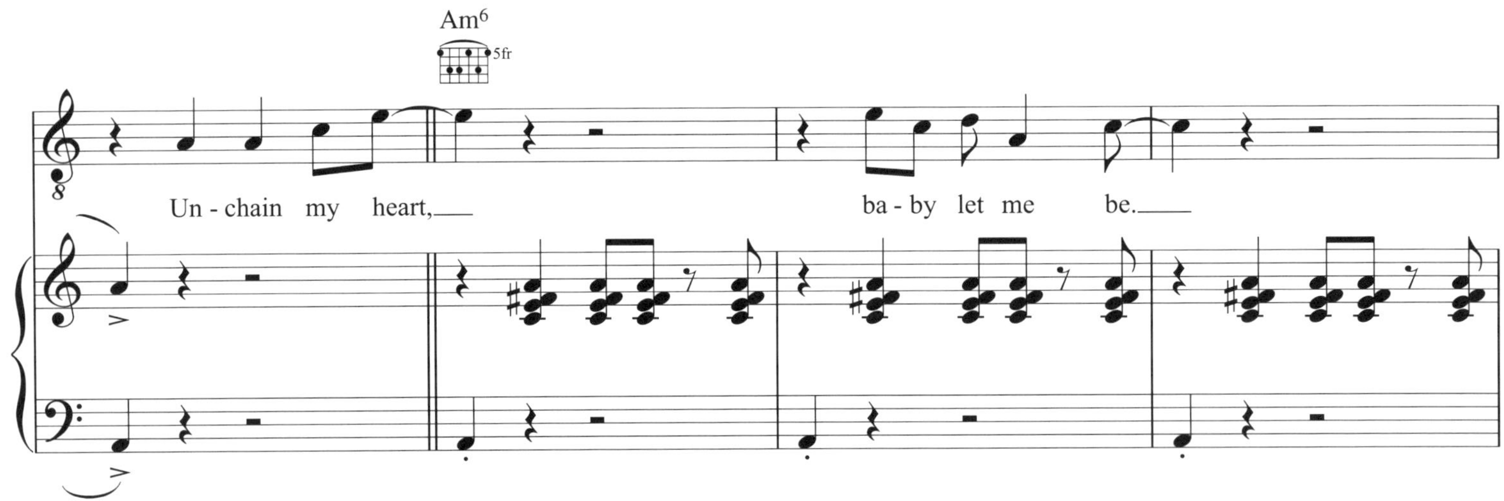

Dm6   Am6
You've got me sewn up like a pil - low case,____
Dm6   Am6   F7
but you let my love go to waste,__ so un - chain____ my heart, oh
E7   N.C.
please please set me free.____   Un - chain my heart,
Am6
ba - by let me go.____   Un - chain my heart,__

F7
Am6 5fr
'cos you don't love me no more.
Dm6 4fr
Am6 5fr
Ev - 'ry time I call you on the phone,
Dm6 4fr
Am6 5fr
F7
some fel - la tells me that you're not at home, so un - chain my heart, oh
E7
N.C.
please, please set me free.
I'm un - der your spell

Dm6
Am6
like a man in a trance,__
but I know darn__
Dm6
F7
E7
N.C.
well__
that I don't stand a chance.
So un-chain my heart,__
Am6
let me go my way.__
Un-chain my heart,__
F7
Am6
you wor-ry me night and day.__

Dm6
Am6
Why lead me through a life of mi - se - ry,
Dm6
Am6
F7
when you don't care a - bout a bean for me, so un - chain my heart, oh
E7
To Coda
N.C.
please, please set me free.
Am6
Sax. solo ad lib.

I'm un-der your spell
Oh won't you set me free?
Woah, set me free.
D.S. al Coda
Coda
Repeat and fade
N.C.

What'd I Say

Words & Music by Ray Charles

2 bars count in   ♩=179

N.C.
3   3   3   3   3
A7
E7   B7
A7   E   B7

E7
N.C.
E7
N.C.
E7
1. Hey ma-ma don't you treat me___wrong,
come and love your dad-dy all night long, al - right___
2. See the girl___ with the dia-mond ring,___
she knows how to shake that thing, al - right___
A7
E7
___ now,
hey,___ hey,
al -
___ now,
hey,___ hey,
al -
B7
A7
E7
1.
B7
-right.
-right.
2.
B7
E7
N.C.
E7
N.C.
E7
N.C.
Tell your ma-ma,
tell your pa,
I'm gon-na send you back to

E7 A7
Ark - an - sas,   Oh_______   yes ma'am,   you don't do___ right,__
E7   B7
___   don't do   right.___
A7   E7   B7
E7   N.C.   E7   N.C.   E7
When you see me in   mi-se-ry,   come on___ ba-by   see a-bout me now, yeah,__

A7
E7
al - right,
B7
A7
al - right.
E
B7
N.C.

E7
N.C.
E7
N.C.
When you see me in mi-se-ry, come on__ ba-by see a-bout me now, yeah,__
A7
E7
Hey,_ hey, al -
B7
A7
E
B7
-right.
E7
N.C.
E7
E7
See the girl with the red dress on, she can do the Bird-land all night_ long,

A7
E7
yeah,   yeah,   what'd I   say,___   al -
B7   A7   E7   B7
-right.   Well,________ tell me what'd I   say,__
E7
___ yeah,   tell me what'd I   say right   now.
Ba - by I wanna know right   now,
A7
Tell me what'd I   say,_______   tell me what'd I   say right now.
and__   I wanna know,______   ba - by I wanna know right now,   yeah.
E7

B7
A7
Tell me what'd I say,____ tell me what'd I say,____
And____ I wanna know,____ said____ I wanna know,____
E7
1.
N.C.
2.
N.C.
____ yeah. And____ and I wan-na know,
____ yeah.
2 bar count in. 1° only
N.C.
Er____________ (er),____________ oh____________ (oh).____________
Er (er), oh (oh), er (er), oh (oh), woah one more time.
Oh baby feel so good,
Oh it's al-right,

E7
Said a - one more time,___ ba - by now,
Make me feel so good,___ now_ yeah.
said that it's all right___ right_ now,

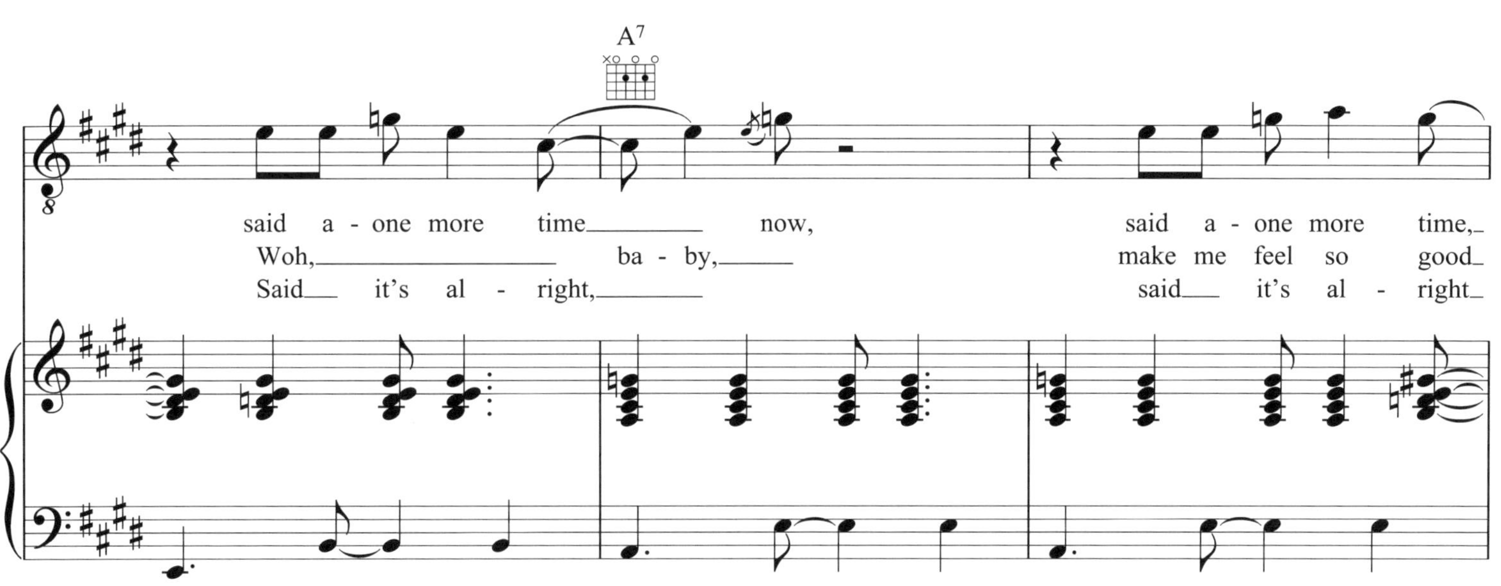

A7
said a - one more time_______ now,
Woh,_____________ ba - by,_____
Said___ it's al - right,_______
said a - one more time,_
make me feel so good_
said___ it's al - right_

E7
___ yeah.
___ yeah.
___ yeah.
B7
Said a - one more time,___
Make me feel so good,___
Said___ it's al - right,___

1, 2, 3.
4.
A7
E7
E7
said a - one more time,_______ yeah.
make me feel so good,_______ yeah.
said__ it's al - right.__
Woh,__
N.C.
E7
__ shake that thing_____ now,
ba - by shake that thing_
A7
__ now now,
ba - by shake that thing,_______
E7
ba - by shake that thing__ right now.
Ba - by shake that thing,_

B7
A7
E7
N.C.
ba-by shake that thing.___ Woh, feel al - right__
E7
__ now yeah, said I feel al - right__ now. Woh,_______________
A7
E7
tell you feel al - right,___ yeah._______ Said I feel al - right,__
B7
A7
E7
__ said I feel al - right._______

123456789

CD Track Listing

Full performance demonstration tracks...

1. Drown In My Own Tears
(Glover) Lark Music Limited.

2. Georgia On My Mind
(Carmichael) Campbell Connelly & Co. Limited.

3. Hallelujah I Love Her So
(Charles) Carlin Music Corp.

4. I Can't Stop Loving You
(Gibson) Acuff-Rose Music Limited.

5. Shake A Tail Feather
(Hayes) Edward Kassner Music Co. Limited.

6. A Song For You
(Russell) Rondor Music (London) Limited.

7. Unchain My Heart
(Powell) Sparta Florida Music Group Limited.

8. What'd I Say (Parts 1 & 2)
(Charles) Carlin Music Corp.

Backing tracks only (without piano)...

9. Drown In My Own Tears
10. Georgia On My Mind
11. Hallelujah I Love Her So
12. I Can't Stop Loving You
13. Shake A Tail Feather
14. A Song For You
15. Unchain My Heart
16. What'd I Say (Parts 1 & 2)

To remove your CD from the plastic sleeve,

Lift the small lip on the side to break the perforated flap.

Replace the disc after use for convenient storage.